AF348571

Published by Canon Press
P.O. Box 8729, Moscow, Idaho 83843
800.488.2034 | www.canonpress.com

Sean Johnson, *Worldview Guide for Anna Karenina*
Copyright ©2017 by Sean Johnson.
For the Canon Classics edition of the novel (2017), visit www.canonpress.com/
books/canon-classics.

Cover design by James Engerbretson
Cover illustration by Forrest Dickison
Interior design by Valerie Anne Bost and James Engerbretson

Printed in the United States of America.

Unless otherwise indicated, Scripture quotations are from the ESV® Bible
(The Holy Bible, English Standard Version®), copyright © 2001 by Crossway,
a publishing ministry of Good News Publishers. Used by permission. All rights
reserved.

A free end-of-book test and answer key are available for download at
www.canonpress.com/ClassicsQuizzes

17 18 19 20 21 22   9 8 7 6 5 4 3 2 1

WORLDVIEW GUIDE

ANNA KARENINA

Sean Johnson

canonpress
Moscow, Idaho

CONTENTS

INTRODUCTION

Anna Karenina is not merely a story, but an argument about which stories are the truest and best. The novel's first words threaten to dissolve all "happy families" into a sea of uninteresting sameness, while unhappy families are unique, intriguing, even romantic. But if the opening line is a universal truth, it is also a challenge Tolstoy sets himself: to shine light on the damnable tragedy that gives unhappiness its luster, and commend the unsung glories of an ordinary life.

THE WORLD AROUND

Leo Tolstoy's other masterpiece, *War and Peace*, had been in print for five years when *Anna Karenina* began to appear in installments in 1875. He was already an established literary celebrity. When the complete novel appeared in print in 1877, he was nearly fifty, and the Russia of his childhood was rapidly transforming. Tsar Alexander II had liberated the serfs in 1861, but the nation still struggled to manage the transition of more than ten million peasants from a slave-like existence under landlords to a free and increasingly autonomous labor force. The transitions were not always smooth or in the best interest of the serfs, and Tolstoy—very much like Levin in the novel—used his position in society to work for improved conditions for the peasant classes.

Growing discontent among the now free peasants as well as philosophical influences from Western Europe were combining to create revolutionary rumblings in

Russia. Marx's *Das Kapital* was translated into Russian in 1872, and in 1881 a group of socialists would succeed in assassinating the tsar. These political currents provide the backdrop for the domestic drama of *Anna Karenina* and reflect Tolstoy's conviction that the breakdown of national peace and social structures is intimately bound up with the breakdown of traditional morality and family structures.

Outside of Russia, Queen Victoria of England had just been declared Empress of India as her nation's imperialistic reach expanded to its zenith. Across the ocean in the U.S., reconstruction was officially ending in the South while the federal government waged war against numerous Indian nations including the tribes of Sitting Bull, Crazy Horse, and Chief Joseph.

ABOUT THE AUTHOR

Count Lev (Leo) Nikolayevich Tolstoy was born into the Russian aristocracy on August 28, 1828. His parents died when he was still young, and he came into his inheritance early. He briefly lived the profligate life of an aristocratic youth before developing the sober moral concerns that would characterize his adulthood.

According to an ancient Greek maxim, "the fox knows many things, but the hedgehog knows one big thing." Isaiah Berlin writes that "Tolstoy was by nature a fox," or a thinker who goes through life pursuing many different "often unrelated and even contradictory" ends, though he "believed in being a hedgehog" and feverishly sought for a single, organizing principle by which he could understand reality and his place in it.[1]

---

1. Isaiah Berlin, *The Hedgehog and the Fox: An Essay On Tolstoy's View of History* (Princeton: Princeton University Press, 2013), 3-4.

The character of Levin in this novel is generally understood to be loosely autobiographical. In addition to sharing Levin's affection for the peasants and peasant life, Tolstoy underwent a spiritual conversion very similar to Levin's as he worked on the novel. After a brief and stormy stint in the Russian church, however, Tolstoy unfortunately became disillusioned with organized Christianity and instead developed his own form of Christian anarchy based upon the moral teachings of Jesus and emphasizing renunciation of the world. With that goal in mind, he moved his family to the country and began to dress and live like a peasant.

Details surrounding his death are debated. It has been said that the eighty-two-year-old, still not satisfied that he was living a properly simple life, wandered away from his estate one winter night with the intention of taking up residence in a monastery. Some say he even reached the monastery and paced the front steps for a long time before his pride got the better of him and he finally went away again. He died on November 7, 1910, in a small train station a day's journey from his home.

WHAT OTHER
NOTABLES SAID

Though the title of "greatest novel" will no doubt remain a disputed point, *Anna Karenina* is often short-listed for the honor. Twentieth-century novelist Vladimir Nabokov complained that Tolstoy was as much a preacher as he was artist, but rejoiced that the artist often won out and produced works like "his immortal *Anna Karenina*."[2] Critic F.R. Leavis called it "*the* European novel."[3]

On the other hand, Victorian thinker Matthew Arnold was of the opinion that in *Anna Karenina* "there are many characters…too many" and that "we are not to take *Anna Karenina* as a work of art; we are to take it as a piece of

2. Vladimir Nabokov, *Lectures on Russian Literature* (New York: Harcourt Brace Jovanovich, 1981), 138.
3. F.R. Leavis, *Anna Karenina and Other Essays* (London: Chatto & Windus, 1967), 32.

life."[4] Henry James also found the novel too crowded and lacking structure—at least the *kind* of structure ("composition" and "architecture") he was fond of building into his own novels: "Tolstoy and Doistoieffsky [sic] are fluid pudding, though not tasteless, because the amount of their own minds and solution in the broth gives it savour and flavour, thanks to the strong, rank quality of their genius and their experience."[5]

And the judgment of Fyodor Dostoevsky's "genius" and "experience"? He hailed it as a great Russian achievement: "*Anna Karenina*, as an artistic production, is perfect."[6] Savor and flavor, indeed.

---

4. Matthew Arnold, *Essays in Criticism* (London: Macmillan and Co., 1865), 412.

5. Henry James, "Letter to Hugh Walpole, May 19, 1912," *The Letters of Henry James*, vol. 2, ed. Percy Lubbock (New York: Charles Scribner's Sons, 1920), 237.

6. Fyodor Dostoevsky, *The Diary of a Writer*, vol. 2, trans. Boris Brasol (New York: Charles Scribner's Sons, 1949), 785.

PLOT SUMMARY, SETTING, AND CHARACTERS

- *Setting: Moscow, St. Petersburg, and the rural provinces surrounding Levin's estate between 1872 and 1876*

- *Anna Arkadyevna Karenina:*[7] the title character; lively and beautiful wife of an older government official

- *Oblonsky, Prince Stepan Arkadyevich ("Stiva"):* Anna's brother; a charismatic and universally

---

7. A note on names: Russian names have always proved notoriously difficult for English translators. Cyrillic letters don't transliterate smoothly into English, Russian last names have masculine and feminine versions so that spouses appear to have different last names, and the concept of taking one's father's name as a middle name is unfamiliar to Americans. Some translators choose to remain as true as possible to the original Russian names while others substitute more familiar Anglicized versions (e.g., "Stephen" for "Stepan" or "Catherine" for "Ekaterina").

liked civil servant who bounces from love affair
to love affair with impunity

- *Dolly (Princess[8] Darya Alexandrovna Oblonska-
  ya):* Oblonsky's longsuffering wife who over-
  looks her husband's infidelities for the sake of
  her children
- *Karenin, Alexey Alexandrovich:* Anna's cold,
  pious husband, who is concerned primarily with
  the opinions of society and their bearing on his
  own reputation and career
- *Levin, Constantine Dmitrich ("Kostya"):* the
  magnanimous and philosophical landlord who
  desires a simple life and is committed to the
  idea of marriage; the novel's co-protagonist and
  in some ways a picture of Tolstoy himself
- *Kitty (Princess Ekaterina Alexandrovna Shcher-
  batskaya):* Dolly's sister; young debutant who is
  initially enamored of Vronsky but later marries
  Levin

---

8. A number of characters have title of nobility in their names: "prince,"
"count," "princess," etc. While the Russian nobility had a rich medieval
past, by the late 1800s many noble families had declined in wealth and
prestige, nobles did not necessarily have civic responsibilities attached
to their ranks, and even the ranks themselves had become confused—
so that a count might be wealthier and more well-to-do than, say, a
prince. As a result, the language of nobility in Russian names in this
period are not so much specific titles as they are indicators of member-
ship in a certain social class.

- *Vronsky, Count Alexey Kirilich:* Suave and unambitious military officer who draws Anna Karenina into an adulterous affair

The plot of *Anna Karenina* is effectively two parallel love stories—one tragic, the other comedic. They run opposite to one another, like two trains passing on the same line; the heroine, Anna, speeding headlong from happiness to tragedy, while the hero, Levin, makes his way from sorrow and isolation toward the very happiness that Anna has abandoned. In the first part, Anna, upright wife and mother, is called to the Petersburg house of her brother Oblonsky to smooth over the aftermath of an adulterous affair recently discovered by his wife. She travels to Moscow by train and at the station has a chance encounter with the wealthy young military officer, Count Vronsky. An instant and unspoken attraction forms between them. In the course of their brief initial meeting, a tragic accident occurs and a man is killed under a train. The death creates in Anna a sense of foreboding, but in the following months she sees Vronsky more and more until they each admit their love for one another and strike up an adulterous affair.

Levin, meanwhile, longs to be married and proposes to his longtime acquaintance, Kitty. Kitty, who is in love with Vronsky, politely but resolutely refuses him, only to be flung into a health-altering depression a few days later when Vronsky and Anna flirt openly at a ball. A year goes by before Levin and Kitty are together again, and Kitty, who has realized her folly in desiring the suave Vronsky over the good and earnest Levin, encourages his attentions anew. The two marry and leave the city to live on Levin's rural estate, where he is engaged in the idealistic venture of revolutionizing Russian agriculture through improved relations between landlords and free peasants. When Levin finds that his new bride requires a great deal of his time and diverts him from some of his labors, he realizes that even his lofty and romanticized view of marriage had not taken his own selfishness into account. This realization makes him, by turns, a more patient and giving husband, and the Levins enjoy a fruitful if unglamorous marriage.

When Anna and Vronsky's affair becomes public knowledge and Anna becomes pregnant, Anna is cast out of her former social circles and her husband punishes her by forbidding the divorce that would let her live openly with her new lover. Thus the two leave Russia and travel Europe until Anna can no longer bear to be away from her son, Serezha. Vronsky proves an inattentive lover and, though he is determined not to abandon Anna, she grows irrationally jealous and ultimately decides to punish his neglect through her suicide. Captivated by the memory of the tragedy she and Vronsky witnessed at their first meeting, she determines to die in the same manner. She throws herself under a train, regrets her decision and utters a prayer for forgiveness, but is struck and killed before she can save herself—cut in two just as she had cut her own family in two.

WORLDVIEW ANALYSIS

Anna Karenina's opening line—equal even to "Call me Ishmael" or "It was the best of times..." in literary greatness—is like a stage director's introduction before the curtain rises and the real drama begins. It stands slightly apart from the paragraphs that follow, like an invitation to let that first sentence unravel the rest of the novel for us: "All happy families resemble one another; but each unhappy family is unhappy in its own way" (1).[9] It is a kind of riddle, and we are meant to ask "Why?" What is

9. The existence of multiple translations may explain why, great as it is, *Anna Karenina*'s opening line is not as familiar in the mouths of English readers. I have cited Louise and Aylmer Maude's 1918 translation, which is one of the best. They were friends of Tolstoy and lived much of their lives in Russia developing interest in his work. During his lifetime, Tolstoy considered their version to be the best existing translation of his novel. Leo Tolstoy, *Anna Karenina*, trans. Louise and Aylmer Maude, ed. George Gibian (New York: W.W. Norton, 1995).

it about happy families that makes them so similar, while unhappy ones are so diverse?

The first clue comes in the intellectual habits of Stephan Oblonsky, himself the head of one of those unhappy families. Oblonsky's opinions and commitments are not grounded in anything objective or permanent. "He firmly held to the opinions of the majority and of his paper on those subjects [science, art, and politics], changing his views when the majority changed theirs,—or rather, not changing them—they changed imperceptibly of their own accord" (6). Oblonsky is the man St. Paul describes in Ephesians 4:14, "carried about by every wind of doctrine" and shifting public opinion. This disposition extends, predictably, into the rest of his life, too. Oblonsky is also carried about by every appetite, every pretty dancer, and every young French governess he encounters, which is precisely why his household is fracturing when we meet him.

Oblonsky's sister, the title character, Anna, follows her passions to even greater ruin than Oblonsky. Tolstoy repeatedly associates her with fluctuation between extreme temperatures—"rapid changes from steaming heat to cold, and back again to heat" (91)—to punctuate her sudden cooling toward her husband and hasty warming toward Vronsky. In the end she will begin to suspect her new lover of the very inconstancy she herself has been guilty of in her marriage, and that jealousy is what drives her to her sorrowful, suicidal end. All of these unhappy lovers confuse their passions for love, and when genuine love eludes them they cannot help but be unhappy.

By contrast, the rare "happy" families in *Anna Karenina* are that way because they are all devoted to the ideal of the family—to an objective reality outside of themselves—rather than to the personal satisfaction that can be found there. Levin's love for Kitty begins, not as a hot passion for a pretty face, but as affection for the whole Shcherbatsky family and their mode of life. Even after his attentions come to rest on Kitty, Levin seems to understand love as something to be aimed at, to be approached, to be participated in. It is, in his mind, "transcending everything earthly, and he … himself so very earthly and insignificant a creature" (20). For Levin, love is a thing greater than himself and he would rather sacrifice his own happiness than be the object of love he doesn't deserve. In contrast, for Vronsky, "love" serves the greater end of his own personal happiness. Though Levin understands the transcendence of love only vaguely in the early chapters of the novel, he ultimately comes to his religious conversion in Part VIII and is able to articulate a unifying purpose for all of life: "To live not for one's needs but for God!" (720). In those words the shared secret of all happy families is revealed. Their common touchstone is the divine love itself. Like siblings who share a strong family resemblance, happy families are all alike because their happiness has the same source.

The unhappiness of the Oblonsky household stems from a husband's inability to ground himself in a transcendent standard for viewing the world and behaving in it. To say that Oblonsky believes in a "subjective morality" might be too simple, but it captures part of the truth. Anna herself will later remark, as she allows herself to entertain the thought of adultery with Vronsky, that "there are as many kinds of love as there are hearts" (125). She might as easily have said that there are as many versions of the law as there are men.

With comments like these, Tolstoy builds an overarching irony against the backdrop of the novel's epigram: "Vengeance is mine; I will repay" (1). Though he leaves the quotation unattributed, the phrase would have been as recognizable to Tolstoy's original audience as it is to us; they are the words of God recorded by Moses in Deuteronomy 32 and quoted by St. Paul in Romans 12. The irony here is of the dramatic variety—it relies on the reader being aware of what some or all of the characters are not. In this case, characters like Anna and her brother forget or deny the existence of a moral law that they are answerable to.

Anna's life, then, will bear out the consistent manifestation of divine punishment as the dissolution of families and the isolation of their members. In their attempts to individuate themselves from moral restrictions, characters like Anna and Oblonsky—even Vronsky—alienate their families or break them entirely, cutting themselves adrift from what Tolstoy paints as society's cardinal institution. Anna's situation is unique, though, and uniquely tragic. Prior to her affair, she is considered by many to be a virtuous woman, and Tolstoy allows us to believe that was, in some sense, truly the case. After she is drawn into infidelity, she cannot wholly suppress her old moral sensibilities and is wracked, on occasion, with the guilt and shame of what she has done. Her guilt not only prevents reconciliation with her husband, but painfully inhibits any true attachment to her new lover as well. True individuals can only enjoy so much of love while they remain *individual*; only within the communal bond of licit marriage are complete trust and sincere passion attainable. Anna truly becomes her own woman, but it is anything but liberating.

In this regard, Anna most resembles Levin, whose pronounced moral sense isolates him from many of his less reflective friends and relations. Levin, we learn, is also tormented by sins in his past, so much so that he insists upon Kitty reading the journals that describe his infidelities before they take their marriage vows. Levin, though, moves steadily out of his loneliness and into the growing community of his young family. Levin's pangs of conscience have driven him away from his sins, while Anna's only drive her deeper into her isolation. That isolation is punctuated by her unequal yoking with the young and uncomplicated Vronsky.

Like Oblonsky, Vronsky's only ethical standard is the progressive opinion of popular society. "He knew very well that he ran no risk of appearing ridiculous…in the eyes of Society people generally… [T]he role of a man who was pursuing a married woman, and who made it the purpose of his life at all cost to draw her into adultery, was one which had in it something beautiful and dignified and could never be ridiculous" (117). And even then it is not condemnation that he risks, but merely "appearing ridiculous." Because Anna and Vronsky's love for one another remains self-focused—merely a parody of the real thing—their relationship, even at its most heated, will remain confusedly dispassionate, and their union imperfect. Even together, they are alone and strangers.

Anna's delayed arrival in the novel also deepens the sense of otherness that surrounds her. We are made to wait seventeen chapters for the appearance of the woman Tolstoy's story is named for—just enough time for characters and readers alike to build up in their minds images of an idealized Anna. Seventeen chapters! Who will she be? Tolstoy encourages us to expect a heroine who will sweep in and restore the domestic felicity of the Oblonksy household. "My sister Anna Arkadyevna is coming to-morrow," Oblonsky rejoices, and "The Lord be thanked!" is his servant's response (4). Does the Anna who eventually materializes fulfill the expectations that have grown up around her, or frustrate them? Even the answer to that question takes time to solidify, and comes only in snapshots.

While contemplating Anna's visit, Dolly reflects on past visits to the Karenin home in St. Petersburg: "She had not liked their house: there seemed to be something false in the tone of their family life" (61). That *something*—the sense of trouble or foreboding that instinct can grasp so well but words can seldom communicate—is a persistent difficulty for Tolstoy's characters, as we will see later. "But why should I not receive her?" Dolly must conclude when she can recall no solid evidence to justify her misgivings (61). And they do seem unfounded when Anna arrives, effortlessly enchants Dolly's children like a Mary Poppins, and seems to repair the fractured Oblonsky marriage—all before lunchtime.

Anna charms Kitty, Dolly's younger sister, too. As they sit together discussing the upcoming ball, Kitty remarks wistfully, "I imagine you at the ball in lilac" (66). Tolstoy's comments about the young Kitty's interest in Anna may explain this very specific imagining: "Kitty felt that Anna was perfectly unaffected and was not trying to conceal anything, but that she lived in another, higher world full of complex poetic interests beyond Kitty's reach" (65). Here Tolstoy introduces the very human problem of the *inner life*—the secret workings of a person's heart and mind that cannot be easily comprehended from the outside. What is the complex, divine-image-bearing creature across the table from you really thinking and feeling? How difficult it is to know for sure! So we often fill in the gaps with what we would like to be true. In Kitty's mind, Anna is an elegant and ageless matron—a faerie-like creature of the daylight—so she naturally associates her with a flower and color that traditionally symbolize innocence and spiritual purity. Kitty must guess at the parts of Anna's nature she cannot see, and she guesses wrongly.

Anna arrives at the ball, "not in lilac, the colour Kitty was so sure she ought to have worn, but in a low-necked black velvet dress which exposed her full shoulders and bosom that seemed carved out of old ivory..." (72). Her revealing gown uncovers more than her shapely figure; it reveals the passion-driven Anna-of-the-evening who, by the time she has left the ball, will have crushed a young girl's dreams of love and embarked on the adulterous trajectory that leads ultimately to her death. Kitty is struck all at once by her mistake in judgment. "She now realized that Anna could not have worn lilac, and that her charm lay precisely in the fact that her personality always stood out from her dress, that her dress was never conspicuous on her. And her black velvet with rich lace was not at all conspicuous, but served only as a frame; she alone was noticeable..." (72). Anna has made herself a work of art; she has chosen an outfit that lays her bare—that frames and displays the complexities of her character not oft seen in her everyday matronly occupations.

Understanding Anna as a character in literature is made easier, in part, if we understand her as a *reader* of literature. Like another literary adulteress—Emma Bovary in Gustave Flaubert's *Madam Bovary*—Anna has an active literary imagination. But, where Madam Bovary reads because she longs to escape into the stories of other people's lives, in Anna's case it is "unpleasant to read" because "she was too eager to live herself" (92), to write the exciting details of stories into her own life. She conceives of herself as the central character of her story, forgetting the bigger story that the epigraph is always subtly pointing the reader back to—the story God is telling. So, Anna begins to put *herself* in frames that propriety may have reserved for another.

The ball in Part I is not the last time Tolstoy speaks of Anna within a "frame." Several literal portraits of Anna provoke discussions of her nature and character throughout the novel.[10] Her husband, Karenin, has a portrait of Anna "by a celebrated artist" in his study (259). We know Karenin is a man of stunted artistic tastes, and he is unable to view the portrait objectively. Instead, the picture that he once found beautiful later only reminds him of Anna's infidelities and his own bitterness toward her, showing him something "intolerably bold and provocative" (259). While Vronsky is living in Europe with Anna, he takes up painting and produces his own portrait of Anna "dressed as an Italian, and he…considered the portrait a great success" (423). Finally, Anna sits for a portrait by the talented

------

10. Eduard Babaev connects the three portraits in his analysis of art theory in the novel, *Essays on Tolstoy's Aesthetics and Literary Works*, trans. George Gibian (Moscow, 1981), 181-86.

but unknown painter, Mikhaylov. Vronsky thinks little of the artist's technical achievements, but is surprised "that Mikhaylov had been able to discover that special beauty…that sweetest spiritual expression" (434) which Vronsky had never noticed, but only glimpsed in the artistic vision of another.[11]

The discrepancy between the latter two portraits connects the problem of the inner life to the challenges of the artist. Vronsky dresses his Anna in Italian costume; he wants to change Anna to fit his particular vision, instead of revealing what is already true (and invisible) about her. Insomuch, Tolstoy marks Vronsky's art a failure (435). His art misses the real Anna because it is selfish, just as his love for her is selfish and consuming. The novel is littered with evidence of this self-focused love, but one of the most striking examples is the similarity between the tragic death of Vronsky's racehorse, Frou Frou, and the bittersweet moment when he finally comes to possess the married woman he has been pursuing. During the steeplechase in Part II Vronsky forgets his concern for his horse's safety and begins to think only of himself winning the difficult race. In the end, he mishandles a jump and inadvertently breaks the animal's back. As the dying creature writhes at his feet, he looks on, "pale and with quivering jaw" (182), lamenting the life he has destroyed. Only

––––––––––

11. The name "Mikhayl" means "gift from God," and may explain what Vronsky misses: presumably anyone can learn technique, but Tolstoy understands artistic *vision* as a gift that only certain souls possess.

weeks before he had stood over a sobbing Anna, having finally consummated their infidelity, "pale, with trembling lower jaw," and feeling "what a murderer must feel when looking at the body he has deprived of life" (135). Even when she is most exposed to him, he can only see what *he* has done to her.

If the Lord says "vengeance is mine" because only he is a fit judge of a person's heart, then only those who see with the eyes of God—those whose love is as unbiased as divine love—can accurately portray a tragic figure like Anna. In the novel, that is Mikhaylov; beyond the novel that is Tolstoy, the creator of the novel itself. Tolstoy wrote in his essay *What Is Art?* that "not only is infection a sure sign of art, but the degree of infectiousness is also the sole measure of excellence in art."[12] The feeling is one of having merged with the artist, of being suddenly struck that he has said or captured just what you have always known yourself but have been unable to say or to show. In short, Tolstoy's "infectiousness" is the power to form the thoughts of the artist in the minds of the audience. Levin, when he glimpses Mikhaylov's painting, is "infected" by the vision of Anna that the portrait presents to him— struck by the revelation of some secret of her inner self— and finds that he can no longer think ill of her, but only pity her. Arguably, the novel is designed to bring its reader to the same point.

---

12. Leo Tolstoy, *What is Art?*, trans. Aylmer Maude (New York: Funk & Wagnalls Company, 1904), 153.

Here is perhaps the final and strongest sense of Tolstoy's epigram at work. Once we have witnessed Anna's sufferings, seen her wracked with the turmoil of guilt, and seen her at her most vulnerable, do we find it in ourselves to withhold our own pity in judgment? Only the reader sees Anna in her final moments, afraid and kneeling, repenting of her suicide and praying "God forgive me everything." Armed with that knowledge, we are hard-pressed to take great satisfaction in her death, and are stung by uncharitable comments made about her by other characters as the novel winds on to its conclusion.

And the novel does, indeed, go on. In the end, Tolstoy the artist is able to reveal to the reader something about Anna that even she fails to recognize about herself—she is radiant, and pitiable, but she is not the center of her world. The novel began without her and will continue without her. It is Levin and Kitty who remain, the faithful lovers who escape the draw of passion and follow real love into the bonds of marriage where their passion is transformed and given back to them. They have developed a distrust of city life with its temptations, extravagances, and preoccupation with salacious affairs. They settle, instead, into a domestic existence close to the peasants and close to the land. Here, Levin resigns himself to the role of a *pater familias* and gentleman farmer.

It is in the midst of these self-effacing duties that a conversation with a peasant convinces Levin it is possible "to live not for one's needs but for God!" (720). In his resulting conversion, Levin realizes the secret of all happy families. There are, he concludes, only two ways to live: for one's needs and desires—which are as numerous as the unhappy families they plague—or for God—who unites all truths and all people in himself.

QUOTABLES

1. All happy families resemble one another, but each unhappy family is unhappy in its own way.

    ~Narrator, 1

2. He soon felt that the realization of his longing gave him only one grain of the mountain of bliss he had anticipated. That realization showed him the eternal error men make by imagining that happiness consists in the gratification of their wishes.

    ~Narrator, about Vronsky, 422

3. "If it is true that there are as many minds as there are heads, then there are as many kinds of love as there are hearts."

    ~Anna, 125

4. He was contented then, but not for long. Soon he felt rising in his soul a desire for desires—boredom.

    ~Narrator, about Vronsky, 422

5. "Without knowing what I am, and why I am here, it is
    impossible to live. Yet I cannot know that, and there-
    fore I can't live"…. And though he was a happy and
    healthy family man, Levin was several times so near to
    suicide that he hid a cord he had lest he should hang
    himself, and he feared to carry a gun lest he should
    shoot himself. But he did not hang or shoot himself
    and went on living.

    ~Levin/Narrator, 714

6. "I shall still get angry with Ivan the coachman in the
    same way, shall dispute in the same way, shall inoppor-
    tunely express my thoughts; there will still be a wall
    between my soul's holy of holies and other people; even
    my wife I shall still blame for my own fears and shall
    repent of it of it. My reason will still not understand
    why I pray, but I shall still pray, and my life, my whole
    life, independently of anything that may happen to me,
    is every moment of it no longer meaningless as it was
    before, but has an unquestionable meaning of goodness
    with which I have the power to invest it."

    ~Levin, 740

21 SIGNIFICANT QUESTIONS AND ANSWERS

1. Describe Anna's character. When and how are her essential qualities revealed?

> Anna is a vibrant and imaginative young woman who reads often and even writes literature for children. When we first meet her, she still enjoys a reputation as a virtuous woman, though she is filled with passions that ultimately get the better of her. The first intelligence about Anna and her character comes from the mouths of others, and she will remain a topic of third-party discussion—slanderous as well as sympathetic—throughout the novel. At several important turns, Anna reveals herself through action: she astounds and alienates Kitty (and, arguably, herself) at the ball by encouraging Vronsky's advances, betrays her love for Vronsky to her husband by her reaction to Frou Frou's fall in the steeplechase, etc. And Anna is revealed to the

reader through her internal thoughts and emotions more than any other character except, perhaps, for Levin.

2. Compare and contrast Levin and Vronsky.

On the morning of her death, Anna says of Vronsky, "What did he look for in me? Not so much love as the satisfaction of his vanity" (690). Unlike the meditative Levin, Vronsky is incapable of real empathy—of looking past his own desires and interests to grasp the inner thoughts, fears, and pains of others. As a result, he pursues Kitty and then Anna for the sake of self-satisfaction, and cannot foresee or will not consider the harm or ruin he may cause them. Levin is the anti-Vronsky, almost despairing of romantic happiness because he fears he cannot love Kitty as she deserves. The moral obligations of love are always before Levin, while Vronsky cannot conceive of a higher cause than his own pleasure.

3. How have Levin and Vronsky, the novel's principal lovers, had their views of love and marriage influenced by their parents?

The very first piece of biographical information the novel offers about Vronsky is that he "had never known family life" (52) and that his mother, an attractive socialite, had many publicized love affairs both before and after her husband's death. As a result, he does not look forward to a family of his own and does not believe marriage has to be bound up in romance. Levin, by contrast, idealizes the marriage of his own parents and the house they kept together. It was "a whole world," a complete cosmos to Levin: "It was the world in which his father and mother had lived and died…and which he had dreamed of renewing with a wife and family of his own" (87).

4. How is Anna's death foreshadowed?

Almost from the moment Anna enters the story, she is connected with death. Her first meeting with Vronsky is punctuated by a man's death under the wheels of a train. She calls the accident "a bad omen" (60), and it ultimately provides the inspiration for her own suicide. Vronsky even feels "what a murderer must feel" after he and Anna first consummate their affair, and feels too that "he must cut this body into pieces and hide it" (149). While she is pregnant, Anna develops an irrational certainty that giving birth to the child—the product of her love of Vronsky—will kill her.

5. Why does Karenin refuse to grant his wife a divorce? What does this reveal about their marriage?

Karenin is supremely concerned with his own professional reputation and, when he learns of his wife's infidelities, offers her a threatening reminder of the hardships a disgraced woman might expect to face without the social and financial protection of a husband. He warns her to keep the affair a secret and continue to play the part of faithful wife, or be disgraced and separated from her beloved son. His firm but subtle threats give way to an all-out refusal to grant her a divorce, and Tolstoy reveals that Karenin's chief motivation is not a desire for reconciliation, but a desire to punish Anna by keeping her from her lover. While these circumstances don't vindicate Anna, they do reveal that the Karenin marriage is, as Nabokov puts it, "as sinful as Anna's love affair is to be"[13] because it is not based on real love or affinity between husband and wife. Karenin isn't heartbroken to learn of the affair, but embarrassed, and does not yearn for the restoration of his wife but desires her suffering.

6. How are cities of Moscow and St. Petersburg contrasted in the novel?

> Moscow, Russia's elder city, was known as a city of churches until the time of the Soviet revolution, and in the 1870s the values of the city were the conservative Christian values of "old Russia." These are seen in Karenin and his strodgy, pietistic circle of acquaintances. They contrast baldly with the progressive set Vronsky runs with in St. Petersburg. Itself an upstart city without roots, built by Peter the Great in a swamp, Petersburg is the center of Europeanization and liberalization in Russia. Its socialites balk at traditional family structures and celebrate brazen affairs, and it is here that Anna is first drawn to Vronsky.

---

13. Nabokov, *Lectures on Russian Literature*, 188.

7. How are rural settings like Levin's estate contrasted with the novel's major cities?

> While Moscow compares favorably to St. Petersburg in the novel, both have their failings. Moscow's Christians are at times painted as hard-hearted or hypocritical, Lydia Ivanovna being a chief example. And the residents of both cities are ever concerned with social climbing and bureaucratic politics. In the country, however, there is a quiet, unpretentious air, so that even a consummate city-dweller like Oblonsky is drawn back there again and again.

8. How are peasants and peasant life depicted in this novel?

> Tolstoy's rural scenes are distinguished most by their inhabitants. The quiet spirit of the country is inseparable from the quiet simplicity of the peasants who dwell there. Levin is frequently frustrated by the laziness of the peasants who work for him, but their flaws still compare favorably to those of the novel's aristocratic city dwellers. For Tolstoy, their closeness to the earth seems to reflect a closeness to God, and it is in the simple, earnest life of peasants that traditional marriage is honored and simple, profound piety is preserved.

9. How do human characters usurp the role of judge and attempt to take vengeance on others in the novel?

The theme of vengeance runs prominently through the novel, starting with the epigraph (*"Vengeance is mine, I will repay"*), and each attempt at vengeance comes across as wrongheaded or petty. Karenin's desire to punish his wife puts him in the place of the avenger, but he is championing no cause but his own. Levin also concludes, after coming to understand Anna, that he was mistaken to have "judged her so severely" (634). But the chief example is that of Anna herself, believing that her suicide will sting Vronsky, punishing him for his inattentiveness.

10. How does polite society's treatment of Vronsky differ from its treatment of Anna after their affair becomes public?

After Anna and Vronsky's affair becomes public knowledge and she leaves her husband's house, Anna is no longer welcome in the social circles she used to frequent. Even calling on Anna or associating with her is more than most of her former friends are willing to do. By contrast, Vronsky remains free to move in the same circles as before, even finding his stock rising in public opinion; after all, his associates find "something beautiful and dignified" (117) in a young man taking up with a married woman. The double standard is a damning reflection of the sliding moral scale of fashionable Russian society, and our attention is directed back to the epigraph as the St. Petersburg socialites judge Anna by a standard that would condemn them too.

11. In Part V, the narrator is critical of Vronsky's artistic endeavors. What are Vronsky's strengths and weaknesses as a painter, and why is Mikhaylov presented as a superior artist?

> Vronksy, we learn, has no trouble developing the technical skills of an artist. "He had a talent for understanding art and imitating it with accuracy and good taste" (423). The idea that he might be something more is a "pleasant delusion," though, because he was "not inspired directly by life, but indirectly by life already embodied in art" (423). Tolstoy's own voice can be heard loudly in the narrator's comments on the subject, and will resemble ideas from later writings like *What is Art?* Unlike Mikhaylov, who does not need mastery of classical forms in order to capture something true in his art, Vronsky lacks the creativity and vision of a true artist.

12. What is Vronsky's attitude toward Anna's son, and what does it reveal about the nature of his love for Anna?

> Vronsky resents Anna's son, Serezha, because of the inconvenience his presence represents. The resentment reveals the counterfeit nature of Vronsky's love: it will never be the familial love of a husband and father.

13. How is the physical consummation of Anna and Vronsky's adultery in Vol. II, Ch. 11 similar to the sin

of Adam and Eve in Genesis—both in the physical
descriptions and the thematic elements of the scene?

> The moment the act is over, the shadow of guilt
> passes between the two and Anna "drooped her
> once proud, bright, but now shame-stricken head"
> and falls at Vronsky's feet crying, "My God! Forgive
> me!" (135). In addition to their physical naked-
> ness, Vronsky also becomes aware of "her spiritual
> nakedness" and, as Adam and Eve felt compelled to
> hide themselves, he feels a desire to cover his crime
> like a murderer might hide the body of his victim.
> And it is in this moment that the promise of death
> enters Anna's world, as she becomes, in every sense,
> a fallen woman.

14. When passion is substituted for proper love in the re-
    lationships of the characters, trouble follows. Does the
    novel condemn passionate desires altogether?

    > Levin, arguably the hero of the novel, is one of the
    > most passionate characters. While passion proves a
    > poor and toxic substitute for sacrificial, life-giving
    > love, "rightly ordered" passions are vital to enliven-
    > ing proper love, like that of Levin for Kitty. Anna
    > and Vronsky's tumultuous relations also suggest
    > that, when mixed with shame and emotional dis-
    > tance, even passion cannot find its fullest expression.

15. Compare and contrast Levin's newfound belief in God
    at the end of the novel with the beliefs and practices

of orthodox Christianity. Does Levin become, broadly speaking, a Christian?

> Following his conversion, Levin asks himself, "but can I believe in all the Church professes?" (724), and seems to conclude that the Church and its dogmas do not contradict or infringe upon what he identifies as a more fundamental "faith." This toleration of the Church as something compatible with but not essential to the Christian life mirrors Tolstoy's own thinking at the time, though in the space of a few years he would regrettably become disillusioned with the institutional Church altogether.

16. Nabokov writes that Vronsky's departure for the battlefront after Anna's death is "the only unfair device in the novel, unfair because too easy, too pat."[14] Do you agree?

> Sending Vronsky out of the picture may be an easy way to tie up his character arc, but it seems in keeping with Vronsky's character that he could extricate himself from the circumstances with such ease and so little grief. Ultimately, though, his departure draws attention back to the epigraph: though some might feel it is *Vronsky* who should end up under a train, or suffering some other appropriate fate, proper vengeance is not doled out according to human wishes.

---

14. Nabokov, *Lectures on Russian Literature*, 145.

17. The title character dies nineteen chapters (an entire volume) prior to the end of the novel. Is this a structural flaw?

> Henry James might say yes, that the novel's continuing for so long without Anna is a typical example of its soupy lack of proper "architecture." On the other hand, if we understand the parallel lives of Anna and Levin as constituting the book's structure, it is consistent that Anna must diminish in order for Levin to increase.

18. Readers and critics alike have complained that some portions of the novel—including several lengthy discussions of agriculture or local politics—aren't necessary to the plot and could have been omitted. What function might these unnecessary or uninteresting passages serve in Tolstoy's overall project?

> Matthew Arnold's description of the novel as less a piece of art than a "piece of life" points us to the realism—the faithfulness to the details and rhythms of real life—Tolstoy achieves by including these sorts of passages. That realism, in turn, highlights the virtues of a character like Levin, who humbly and contentedly endures the plain or tedious occurrences of life, over and against one like Anna, who is often not content to live anything less than the charmed life of a literary heroine.

19. Do you think the plot of *Anna Karenina* would still work if it were set in the 21st century?

Given the existence of no-fault divorce laws and the high rate at which Americans divorce, imagining a present-day Anna in similar circumstances is difficult. In fact, we can easily picture her reimagined as an empowered heroine gaining freedom from her loveless marriage and discovering she can make it on her own. Nevertheless, Tolstoy's emphasis on society's need of stable, "happy" families is truer and more relevant now than when the novel was first written.

20. In addition to the epigraph, are there any significant biblical images or themes running through the story?

Contrasted with the imagery of Anna and Vronsky's "Fall" scene is language comparing Levin to an unfallen Adam: "He himself felt painfully…that it is not good for a man of his age to be alone" (137, cf. Gen. 2:18). The theme of Levin as a kind of Adam is born out later in the novel, too, by his willingness to take responsibility for his land and to work on it himself, as well as by the fruitful multiplication of his own family.

21. Is Anna repentant in her final moments? Is her dying prayer enough for her to be saved?

20th century British novelist Graham Greene, in his own story about a suicide, has a priest remark that "You can't conceive, my child, nor can I or anyone the…appalling…strangeness of the mercy of God."[15] If we have followed the argument of Tolstoy's novel, we may be able to echo those words with regard to Anna's ultimate fate. Is she sincere? Is she repentant? We might reflect, as St. Augustine did, that there is one instance of death-bed repentance recorded in Scripture—that of the penitent thief on the cross—that no one should utterly despair, and only one, that no one should presume. Perhaps certainty, then, is too much to hope for in such a circumstance. But if Anna's mysterious brightness has worked on us, the read-ers, as it works on Levin and others, then we may, at least, pray that her own frightened prayer gets a favorable hearing.

---

15. Graham Greene, *Brighton Rock* (New York: Penguin Books, 2004), 268.

FURTHER DISCUSSION AND REVIEW

Master what you have read by reviewing and integrating the different elements of this classic.

SETTING AND CHARACTERS

Be able to compare and contrast the personalities (including strengths, weaknesses, and mannerisms) of each character. How does the setting affect the characters?

PLOT

Be able to describe the beginning, middle, and end of the book along with specific details that move the plot forward and make it compelling. This includes the success or downfall (or both) of each character.

CONFLICT

Go through the character list and describe the tension between any and all main characters. Then, think about whether any characters have internal conflict (in their own minds). Is there any overt conflict (fighting), or conflict with impersonal forces?

THEME STATEMENTS

Be able to describe what this classic is telling us about the world. Is the message true? What truth can we take from the plot, characters, conflict, and themes (even if the author didn't believe that truth)? Do any objects take on added meaning because of repetition or their place in the story (i.e., do any objects become symbols)? Be able to explain the following themes (or any others you've noticed) in this classic:

> While the city corrupts Anna, Vronsky, and perhaps Karenin, Levin and Kitty find rejuvenation in the country. Man was meant to live close to the land, to work with his hands, and not to spend his days in idle society.

> Unchecked passion destroys lives and must sometimes be sacrificed, but a mere sense of duty, such as Karenin has, is not enough. Duty must be supported by love and affection.

> True art is infectious, and expresses in a more articulate way something beneath the surface that we already think or feel, perhaps unconsciously.

A NOTE FROM THE PUBLISHER:
TAKING THE CLASSICS QUIZ

Once you have finished the worldview guide, you can prepare for the end-of-book test. Each test will consist of a short-answer section on the book itself and the author, a short-answer section on plot and the narrative, and a long-answer essay section on worldview, conflict, and themes.

Each quiz, along with other helps, can be downloaded for free at www.canonpress.com/ClassicsQuizzes. If you have any questions about the quiz or its answers or the Worldview Guides in general, you can contact Canon Press at service@canonpress.com or 208.892.8074.

ABOUT THE AUTHOR

Sean Johnson is a humanities teacher at Trinitas Christian School in Pensacola, Florida. He took his bachelor's degree in liberal arts and culture from New Saint Andrews College and holds a Master's degree in English Literature from the University of Dallas. He and his wife Heather have two sons.

Made in United States
North Haven, CT
29 January 2024